# Services *for the* urban poor

# Services *for the* urban poor

## 1.

## Guiding Principles

*Andrew Cotton & Kevin Tayler*

Water, Engineering and Development Centre
Loughborough University
2000

Water, Engineering and Development Centre,
Loughborough University,
Leicestershire, LE11 3TU, UK


© A.P. Cotton and W.K. Tayler, 2000

ISBN 13 Paperback: 978 0 90605 578 6
ISBN Ebook: 9781788533430
Book DOI: http://dx.doi.org/10.3362/9781788533430

A catalogue record for this book is available from the British Library.

A reference copy of this publication is also available online at:
http://www.lboro.ac.uk/wedc/publications/sftup.htm

Cotton, A.P. and Tayler, W.K. (2000)
*Services for the Urban Poor:*
*Section 1. Guiding Principles*
WEDC, Loughborough University, UK.

WEDC (The Water, Engineering and Development Centre) at Loughborough University
in the UK is one of the world's leading institutions concerned with education, training,
research and consultancy for the planning, provision and management of physical
infrastructure for development in low- and middleincome countries.

This edition is reprinted and distributed by Practical Action Publishing.
Since 1974, Practical Action Publishing has published and disseminated books and
information in support of international development work throughout the world. Practical
Action Publishing trades only in support of its parent charity objectives and any profits are
covenanted back to Practical Action (Charity Reg. No. 247257, Group VAT Registration No.
880 9924 76).

This document is an output from project R7292 funded by the UK Department for
International Development (DFID) for the benefit of low-income countries.
The views expressed are not necessarily those of DFID.

# Acknowledgements

The financial support of the Department for International Development of the British Government is gratefully acknowledged. The authors would particularly like to thank their many urban engineering colleagues and friends throughout India, Pakistan and Sri Lanka with whom they have worked for the last fifteen years. Their experience has been central to the preparation of this work. Mr P Srinivasa Rao from Hyderabad, India provided a critical review of earlier drafts and additional material for Sections 4 and 6. Colleagues at WEDC and GHK Research and Training provided information and comments throughout the development of the work. We also acknowledge the inclusion of some material from earlier work jointly authored with Dr Richard Franceys. Finally, we wish to acknowledge Sue Cotton for her editorial contributions and the patience and skill of Rod Shaw and Glenda McMahon of the WEDC Publications Office in the design and production of the manual.

# Contents

# Section 1

# Guiding Principles

## Who should read this

Officials of donor/lending agencies and their partners in national and state level government ministries and departments who propose to identify programmes for improving services for the poor in towns and cities.

## Objectives of this section

To present an overview of principles and offer guidance for the development of an action planning approach to improve services for the urban poor within a policy context which supports administrative decentralisation and involvement of users in the planning process.

## What this section tells you

The local **policy context** is fundamental to what can be achieved through action planning; high level policy support from state/national government is an essential 'driver' for more decentralised approaches to planning which accept the importance of involving users in the process.

Potential **benefits** from improving services for the urban poor include: improved health; improved living environment; greater convenience; sounder household finances; opportunities for income generation and skills development.

Many service improvements will be achieved through better **operation and maintenance** rather than construction of new works; from the outset of the planning process it is essential to consider how the O&M of new infrastructure will be managed.

The urban poor are primary **stakeholders**. Key secondary stakeholders are: National and State government; municipalities; local elected Councillors; urban development authorities; specialist line agencies; CBOs; NGOs; the private sector; and external donor/lending agencies.

**Networked services** require external supporting infrastructure to deliver services to the user. **Non-networked services** at the neighbourhood and household level can be developed independently of municipal services through local action alone.

There are different **options for managing urban services**: central management by an institution with statutory responsibility for service delivery; local neighbourhood management by a group of service users; and householder management for privately owned on-plot facilities. Roles and responsibilities need to be clearly defined.

**Quality of service** is of primary concern to users; detailed consideration must be given to their views and preferences. Find out what they want and what they are willing to pay for.

**Women** play a key role as service providers and have specific needs which must be taken into account.

External **finance for subsidies** needs to be carefully targeted: focus on subsidies which benefit the wider community of users, or support 'software' activities such as sanitation promotion. Some mechanisms such as setting cost ceilings may encourage residents to contribute towards higher levels of service.

Ensure that **appropriate technical options** are available as a means of responding to what people want.

**Action planning** centres around understanding what is already happening locally and building on this by working through existing structures. Action planning is not just a technical process; plans must fit into the local institutional and political context.

The proposed action planning approach comprises: **Local Action Plans**, through which the urban poor articulate their demands for improved services; **Action Plans for networked services** which deal with improvements to supply through town/city infrastructure networks; and a process of **consensus building** to gain widespread acceptance amongst stakeholders.

## Policy context

The integration of participatory approaches at the local neighbourhood level with strategic improvements to city level infrastructure is fundamental to the action planning approach for improving services for the urban poor which this manual describes. It is basically about 'service linkages' through networked infrastructure between neighbourhoods and the wider city systems. Experience shows that whilst there are many initiatives undertaken by local people in their own neighbourhoods, these are often constrained because of the difficulty of joining up to the infrastructure outside the neighbourhood. This may be because the main lines are some way off, but this is by no means always the case. The widespread, underlying problem is that improvements made by government are often done in a piecemeal and uncoordinated way which cannot build on or absorb those locally initiated improvements. Whilst lack of resources is often a problem, the main reason is that there is no systematic approach to planning.

The local institutional and political context is of central importance to what can be achieved; this has the following implications for the wider policy context:

■ there needs to be a commitment within municipal government to improve services for the poor which has higher level policy support from state/ central government; and

■ this policy needs to support a more decentralised approach to planning which accepts the importance of involving users in the process.

The extent to which these conditions exist is highly variable. Without these 'policy drivers' it is very unlikely that the potential benefits from improved planning of services will be realised; they can provide the necessary incentive for planning approaches to change. External donor and lending agencies can play an important role in promoting these principles in order to create an environment in which the more strategic approaches to planning outlined in this manual can be implemented effectively.

In most situations a lot of preparatory work will be required in order to convince local officials firstly of the importance of involving users in local planning and secondly in developing a more integrated approach to city wide planning.

See WELL, *Guidance Manual on Water Supply and Sanitation Programmes*, Section 3.1 page 227 concerning policy development.

## Why improve urban services?

This manual is concerned with the following urban services:

- water supply;
- sanitation;
- drainage;
- access and paving;
- street lighting and power supply;
- solid waste management; and
- community buildings.

Improving services for the urban poor has a number of distinct benefits which contribute towards poverty reduction.

- **Health**: increasing the quantity of water used, improving sanitation, removing pools of stagnant water, improving the effectiveness of solid waste collection and removal all contribute to better environmental health providing that the physical improvement measures are complemented by health and hygiene education.

- **Convenience**: saving time through better access to services, improved reliability, greater privacy through improved sanitation, improved mobility and links to the city through better streets and paving.

- **Financial:** households may spend less money on services, e.g. purchasing water from vendors such as better-off households with formal water connections, and paying to use sanitation facilities.

- **Income generation** and enterprise: direct financial benefits can accrue to householders and local business if community groups or local micro-contractors are involved in implementing some of the works. Paving and drainage improves the quality of space around the household which can be used for enterprise activities.

- **Skills development**: involving local groups in the implementation presents opportunities for training in basic construction skills and the associated administrative skills such as basic record keeping and book keeping.

- **Local environment**: measures which tackle problems of liquid and solid waste create a cleaner and healthier local environment. Environmental degradation is particularly bad in low lying areas with ponds and other water-pockets; these can be transformed into attractive features, helping to engender that sense of civic pride and ownership which is crucial to long term sustainability.

## Improving urban services: sustainability

Sustainability is currently one of the top items on many development agendas. In the context of this manual, sustainability is about the operation and maintenance of installed facilities and the ability to draw on their benefits continuously over their useful life. It has important technical, financial, social and institutional dimensions. Many service improvements will be achieved through better O&M rather than construction of new works.

*Operation* refers to the procedures and activities involved in the actual delivery of services, for example, abstraction, treatment, pumping, transmission and distribution of drinking water. *Maintenance* refers to activities aimed at keeping existing capital assets in serviceable condition, for example, repair of water distribution pipes, pumps and public taps.

Always improve the operation and maintenance of the existing infrastructure to get the maximum possible out of what is already there. This forms an essential part of any Action Plan to improve services. All too frequently the tendency is to build something new rather than to investigate how to improve the management of what already exists. This applies equally to local neighbourhood services and town/city infrastructure. Throughout this manual we emphasise the importance of improving O&M alongside identifying the need for new construction. The key issue is that O&M is an essential consideration from the very beginning of the planning process; it is not something which comes in at the end. There is an old adage which is as true today as ever before: 'Do not build what you are capable of building; only build what you are capable of operating and maintaining'.

## Who are the stakeholders?

The primary stakeholders are the urban poor households who are the intended users of the improved services.

There exists a wide range of secondary stakeholders; typical roles and responsibilities are set out in Table 1.1.

## Table 1.1.  Typical stakeholder roles and responsibilities

| Secondary stakeholder | Typical roles and responsibilities |
|---|---|
| National and/or State Government | <ul><li>Setting the broad policy framework incorporating: planning and design standards; cost recovery; subsidy. This has a direct impact on proposed externally funded programmes.</li><li>Coordination of policy to avoid ending up with conflicting messages at the municipal level which then creates confusion and difficulty in implementation.</li><li>Funding specific programmes in infrastructure, health and education.</li></ul> |
| Local Government (Municipalities) | <ul><li>Statutory responsibility for a wide range of service provision including operation and maintenance.</li><li>Specific groups of employees can be affected and may merit separate attention as a distinct stakeholder group e.g. solid waste workers.</li></ul> |
| Local Councillors | <ul><li>Formally elected representatives of the town or city, often controlling a significant proportion of town revenues for spending on local improvement works. An essential group who are often excluded by externally funded programmes either by accident or deliberately.</li><li>Key O&M functions relating to solid waste collection, drain cleaning and street sweeping are often managed directly by Councillors.</li><li>Neglect of this group may result in lack of coordination and duplication.</li></ul> |
| Urban Development Authorities (UDAs) | <ul><li>These exist in many large urban centres and have frequently been selected as the key partner for implementing urban service improvement programmes.</li><li>Sustainability: the new assets often have to be handed over to the municipality for O&M, as the UDAs have neither the resources nor the remit for this.</li></ul> |
| Specialist line agencies | <ul><li>These include agencies with responsibilities for water supply and power supply.</li><li>The extent of their jurisdiction over different parts of the networks varies widely from place to place and it is important that this is established during project identification.</li></ul> |

| Table 1.1. continued | |
| --- | --- |
| **Secondary stakeholder** | **Typical roles and responsibilities** |
| Community Based Organisations (CBOs) | ■ Often engaged in self-help activities, campaigning for better services and in some cases procuring services (see private sector below).<br>■ It is important to take account of existing CBOs before setting up new structures to deal with externally funded programmes.<br>■ Inadequate representation of women and disadvantaged groups may be a concern in some CBOs. |
| Non Government Organisations (NGOs) | ■ Variety of large and small groups including those associated with churches, religious activities and schools.<br>■ Act as intermediaries, negotiating with urban government on behalf of communities.<br>■ Undertake wider advocacy on more equitable service distribution and poverty reduction.<br>■ May be involved directly with service delivery, taking on the role of contractors. |
| Private Sector | ■ Households and community groups engage in informal service provision in the absence of the public sector.<br>■ Small entrepreneurs operating in the informal economy, such as local solid waste collection.<br>■ Formal sector companies providing services such as water supply and solid waste collection to part or all of the town. |
| External donor/ lending agencies | ■ Provision of grant-in-aid or loan finance to support programmes specifically targeting the urban poor.<br>■ Institutional development and technical support programmes influencing pro-poor policies linked to broader policy reform e.g. for increased cost recovery. |

## Networked and non-networked infrastructure

The ways in which services can be planned, managed, operated and maintained is strongly dependent upon whether the infrastructure is networked. In order to deliver the service to the user, networked services require supporting infrastructure which is external to the household and neighbourhood. These can be classified into 'feeder' and 'collector' networks.

Examples of feeder networks include:

- piped water supply; and
- power supply.

Examples of collector networks include:

- main drainage;
- solid waste collection; and
- sewered sanitation.

Non-networked services at the neighbourhood and household level can be developed independently of municipal services *through local action alone*; these include:

- wells and handpumps;
- unsewered sanitation;
- local drainage to soakpits or ponds; and
- solid waste disposal in pits.

In order to develop coherent Action Plans, we need to recognise that there exists a hierarchy in networked infrastructure. It is common to distinguish between *primary, secondary and tertiary* infrastructure as illustrated in Figure 1.1. The key point is that we cannot plan and design tertiary (neighbourhood) level services in isolation; the tertiary level services depend upon the capacity of secondary and primary networks to feed to and collect from the neighbourhood.

## Managing urban services

Traditionally, services have been managed by the public sector; however, we can identify three different systems of management which are illustrated in Table 1.2 by examples from water supply and sanitation.

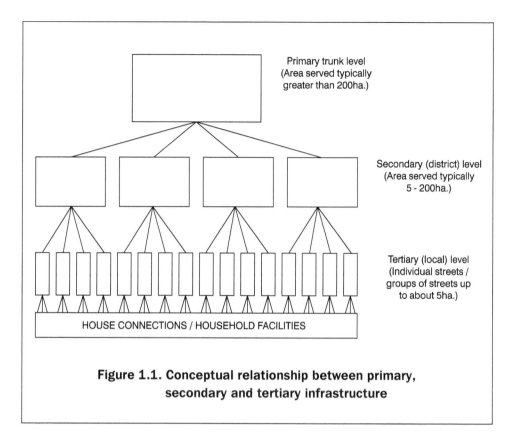

**Figure 1.1. Conceptual relationship between primary, secondary and tertiary infrastructure**

**Table 1.2. Management systems**

| Management system | Examples using water and sanitation |
|---|---|
| *Centrally managed*<br>■ Private service connections to individual plots which require supporting networked infrastructure | ■ Piped water supply<br>■ Sewerage |
| *User group managed*<br>■ Non-private facilities which are shared by members of a user group; depending on the technology adopted, these may or may not require supporting networked infrastructure | *With networked infrastructure*<br>■ Piped water to public standposts<br>■ Sewered communal or shared latrines<br><br>*Without networked infrastructure*<br>■ Communal handpumps or wells<br>■ Communal latrines linked to pits or septic tanks |
| *Householder managed*<br>■ Private on-plot services which do not require supporting networked infrastructure | ■ On-plot wells, handpumps<br>■ Latrines linked to on-plot pits or septic tanks |

Experience shows that there is a whole spectrum of approaches; the essential differences relate to the degree of involvement of the user community, the role of different public sector institutions and tiers of government, and the involvement of the private sector. Each of these three systems clearly has different implications for both implementation and the management of O&M, as shown in Table 1.3.

**Table 1.3. Implications of different management systems**

| Management system | Implications |
|---|---|
| Centrally managed | Public institutions have statutory responsibility for service delivery and O&M either directly or through their private sector contractors. |
| User group managed | A group of users is responsible for service delivery and O&M; if there is external support infrastructure, roles and responsibilities for O&M need to be carefully defined between the community and external agencies. |
| Householder managed | Responsibility for service delivery and O&M of privately owned on-plot facilities rests with the owner/plot holder. Comparatively speaking, this presents few concerns with respect to the management of O&M. |

## Focus on services rather than infrastructure

Users are concerned with the *quality of service* which is available to them. For example, what they want is access to sufficient water of a reasonable quality; the pipes, standposts and handpumps, that is, the *infrastructure*, are no more than mechanisms to deliver the service. It is therefore important to address *overall service provision* as opposed to just the construction of physical infrastructure. This requires a much greater emphasis on the views and preferences of the users, which is quite different from the way in which many public sector institutions are used to working. This focus on service can also be used to create a greater concern for improved O&M.

This has important implications for monitoring and evaluation; the traditional measures of physical construction and financial disbursement do not necessarily tell us whether the intended benefits are being achieved. We need to use participatory methods to explore how the service users are benefiting from the improved services.

## Why involve people with service provision?

It is important to focus on the quality of service; this means finding out about and responding to the perceptions, priorities and preferences of the users. However, this has rarely been the case in programmes where physical improvements to urban infrastructure have been planned and implemented exclusively by professional engineers, planners and architects working to fixed standards and norms. This supply-based approach allows little scope for effective participation of the users, particularly the poor, who have essential knowledge to contribute not least because they know what they want rather than having others decide for them. There is an important proviso here, namely willingness to pay and the available resources which constrain choice; these are considered in the following sections.

The rationale for user participation in planning of services includes the following:

- the services provided are appropriate to the needs and demands of users;

- users may be more willing to contribute to the cost of something they actually want; this can lead to reduced costs for the providing agency;

- services and service providers become more responsive and accountable to users;

- sustainability in terms of recovering costs for O&M is likely to be greater; and

- the activities involved in developing the participation of users can themselves be empowering, through the strengthening of local organisations and their capacity to act on behalf of residents.

There is no blue print method for the optimum level of involvement of users. The key point is that the level of involvement needs to match the local situation and be rooted in a clear understanding of what community members are willing and able to do and to pay for.

## Demand based approaches

Involving users in the planning of services is a means of finding out about demand. However, it is pointless simply to ask users "what they want" because the natural response is to want everything, yet there are only limited resources available. A key objective of local action planning is to be demand responsive, thereby finding out from users *what do you want?* and *how much are you willing to pay for it?* The service provider then supplies the service to satisfy the demand of the user, who pays accordingly.

Some important issues arise around the 'willingess to pay' approach.

- Whilst the urban poor may indicate a high willingness to pay for services such as water, this absorbs a far greater proportion of household income than for better off households. There is little non-essential expenditure, and payment of high charges may be made at the expense of the food budget, which has implications for nutritional status.

- Demand for some services such as water and power supply may be quite apparent, and reflected in a willingness to contribute towards the costs. However, users may indicate a low willingness to pay for other services such as sanitation, drainage and solid waste removal which have very important impacts on environmental health and the quality of the local environment. Users, like anybody else, 'know what they know' and are unlikely to ask for things outside their own experience. It is therefore important to consider the *generation of demand* for other services; for example, sanitation promotion. Some of these programme components are likely to be high on the agenda of local implementing agencies and external donors.

- There may be significant equity implications if it is proposed to recover all of the costs including the capital cost of implementation, the recurrent cost of O&M, and the replacement cost for replacing the facilities when they reach the end of their useful life. Why should programmes targeted at the poor aim for full cost recovery when the better-off are in receipt of services which are highly subsidised in relation to the household charges which are levied?

This is not to argue against cost recovery; rather, it is to appreciate that demand can be interpreted in a wider way than just as an economic mechanism which can otherwise tend to give an over-simplistic view of the problems and solutions. Cost recovery, particularly of the recurrent costs for O&M, helps to improve the financial performance of the municipality and specialist line agencies. Whilst this does not on its own guarantee better services for the poor, by putting these institutions on a sounder financial footing, they at least have more options open to them in terms of improving service delivery. There is a need to view the financial policies and performance of municipalities and the specialist line agencies with a view to reform, in order to avoid further disadvantaging the urban poor.

Within the context of donor programmes which provide financial assistance to improving services for the urban poor it is extremely important to establish mechanisms which reflect demand in its broadest sense. For further guidance on the techniques and their application, refer to the DFID *Guidance Manual on Water Supply and Sanitation Programmes,* (WELL 1998) page 39. Note that participatory methods have a key role to play.

## External finance and subsidy

There are several different approaches which can be considered for programmes which provide external finance for improving services for the urban poor.

- Minimise subsidies which improve on-plot facilities as households can fund these themselves; focus on service improvements which benefit the wider community. This is relatively straightforward for water supply, where communal supplies are a realistic option. It is not so simple for sanitation, where the best options are household latrines; communal latrines have a poor record (this issue is considered later).

- Subsidies can be further limited to improvements to town/city systems with the local neighbourhood improvements being paid for by users. An important issue here is that there may be a low demand for some services which can have a significant impact.

■ Target the subsidy towards 'software' such as promotional activities for sanitation, health and hygiene which might generate increased demand and willingness to pay, rather than constructing infrastructure.

■ Adopt a matching grant system, whereby users contribute a proportion of the capital cost of local neighbourhood improvements. This can be administratively complex and mechanisms need to be in place to deal with cost overrun.

■ Adopt an overall cost ceiling for a particular community; this budget prescribes the limits within which the users can decide their priorities between the different service sectors and the nature or 'level' of service they want. It is discretionary, and can reflect a desire for high levels of service in some sectors with correspondingly lower levels in others. This can be quite complex to develop, but it is workable. One approach is to create a broad classification of the areas to be upgraded; then estimate the indicative cost to bring a sample from each of the classifications up to a very basic level of service (see the following section). Major works such as flood protection can be considered outside of this discretionary budget so that vulnerable communities are not further disadvantaged.

■ Whilst programmes should not fund recurrent costs directly, supporting institutional changes which lead to improved O&M can have significant impact. Systems which cannot recover their O&M costs are always likely to be vulnerable to deteriorating service delivery; users do not then get what they wanted and thought they were paying for.

■ Create a loan fund against which householders and community groups can borrow to improve facilities; however, there is a danger that the poorest will be excluded. Easier access to finance is an important complementary activity to the promotion of sanitation.

■ Residents always have the option to increase their contributions to achieve higher levels of service.

None of these are without their problems; the fundamental difficulty is that some *a priori* decision has to be made about what are 'reasonable' investments and levels of service. This can be explored during the preparatory stages using participatory methods.

One of the key roles of action planning at the municipal level is to coordinate the different sources of finance which are available locally, from state/national government programmes, external donors and possibly the private sector. These can be converged into the upgrading programme and used in an optimum way to avoid piecemeal improvements.

## Levels of service

Local action planning needs to be *demand responsive*. However, traditional approaches to service provision which have exclusively involved professionals in the planning and implementation have usually been "supply driven", based on the adoption of universal norms and standards. These are done on an *a priori* basis without reference to the specific situation other than through general and rather unhelpful classifications such as 'urban', 'middle income' and the like. The result is that city wide 'blue print' solutions are proposed, where everybody in the same category, for example 'slum', gets the same hardware solution regardless of their demand.

This confuses the objectives with the means. Locally appropriate *levels of service* are required which are linked to demand. This can best be dealt with in terms of objectives rather than specifying specific items of hardware. Table 1.4 proposes objectives for each service sector.

| Table 1.4. Service objectives | |
|---|---|
| **Sector** | **Objective** |
| Water supply | Improve reliability, availability, quantity and quality of water |
| Sanitation | Sanitary latrines available for individual households or clearly defined user groups |
| Flood protection | Reduce frequency and duration of flooding |
| Access and paving | Improve all-weather pedestrian access |
| Drainage | Improve removal of sullage and stormwater |
| Solid waste management | Increase storage facilities and collection frequency |
| Power/lighting | Provide increased levels of security lighting |
| Community hall | Improve availability of space suitable for community activities |

These are not tied to fixed items of hardware, but can be interpreted in terms of different hardware options in different circumstances, and give a framework against which the achievements of a particular project component can be judged. It leaves plenty of scope for flexibility as far as specific details of improvements are concerned, and provides a framework within which users' preferences covering a wide range of options can be accommodated. Users can choose different levels of service in different sectors according to their priority and willingness to pay. Cost ceilings in donor financed urban service programmes could realistically be guided by the proposed *basic level* of service. Demand based approaches related to different levels of service involves spending a lot of time and effort with communities in working out the implications of different levels of service.

## Gender issues

Women are largely responsible for accessing services such as water for their families. Improvements to services therefore have a particular impact on the time, effort and money which women spend on these activities. Local Action Plans must reflect the fact that:

■ women have these responsibilities;

■ women know more about the problems of accessing services than men;

■ focusing on the priorities of women is necessary if the health and social benefits of service improvements are to be realised;

■ there are specific needs, particularly related to privacy, which have to be recognised and incorporated into service plans.

However, it must be recognised that women are already busy with childcare, domestic tasks and income generating activities. There is a risk that they can become overburdened with the additional work arising through their recruitment as 'voluntary' community mobilisers and healthworkers. The best way to deal with this is to involve women directly in decision-making from the outset and for implementing agencies to employ women in positions where they can influence programming decisions.

# Action planning

The purpose of action planning is to develop a coherent set of plans which:

- respond to local demand; and

- can be implemented within the local context.

Section 3 of the manual is devoted to the development of Action Plans; the focus of attention is on how these difficult concepts can be made operational by local officials working in the project towns and cities. An important part of the approach is to *understand what is already happening*, and to build on this by working as far as possible through structures and systems which are already there.

At the neighbourhood (tertiary) level, certain options are self contained; examples include the use of wells for water supply, and various forms of on-plot sanitation such as improved pit latrines and septic tanks. For other options which depend on feeder/collector infrastructure, we must know the capacity of the secondary and primary system components in order to plan and design the tertiary level services. It is important to identify whether these capacities are adequate in order to determine if improvements to the second-ary or primary systems are necessary. For example, providing additional community taps does not make more water available unless the secondary networks have the capacity to deliver. We need a clear planning strategy for infrastructure which is coordinated at the city level.

We define three parts to the action planning process.

- *Local action planning* is the mechanism through which the urban poor articulate their demands for improved services. It contains information on the nature and form of the service which the users want and to which they are prepared to allocate the resources at their disposal. This information defines what is needed in terms of tertiary level infrastructure.

- *Network service planning* defines how the services can be supplied in or-der to match the demand which is expressed in the Local Action Plan. The Network Service Plans focus on the capacity of different parts of the pri-mary and secondary infrastructure networks, the additional demands which will be made on them as identified in the Local Action Plans and on actions necessary to upgrade different parts of the systems. Network Service Plans are drawn up on an area-wide basis, working at the municipal Ward level; these are then coordinated at the town/city level for each infrastructure sector.

- ***Consensus Building*** is the key to the planning process and the most difficult part of all. It recognises the need to link together local and municipal
  plans; planning is not just a technical process, but one which, if it is to be
  successful, has to fit into the local institutional and political context. This
  process needs to involve the urban poor users (perhaps with the support of
  intermediaries), officers of the municipality and political representatives of
  the municipality. It brings together the two plans in a context which is necessary to promote the long term sustainability of change and is the only way
  that new approaches can be institutionally learned and absorbed.

A crucial part of the action planning process is therefore about the practicalities
of balancing demand for services at the local level with the supply capacity of
the networked city systems. This must also include a realistic assessment of
the extent to which the city wide systems are likely to be upgraded and
extended. There is an important practical point to make here: it may not prove
possible to satisfy all of the demand for services which are in the Local Action
Plans. This is where the *consensus building* component of action planning
comes to the fore; plans are no use unless they are achievable.

## Risks

One of the major risks in any planning process is that it becomes too complex
to be handled by the local institutions responsible for upgrading even if the
wider policy context is supportive. This is particularly true of programmes
which aim to integrate a whole range of interventions in different sectors (e.g.
health, education, infrastructure) and the difficulties emerge both in local
level planning and planning at the city level. Whilst fully integrated planning
is theoretically essential to obtain maximum benefits, the reality is different,
and we have to break planning down into manageable units. In creating a
manageable planning framework which can be handled at the level of a small
city or a large town in South Asia, we need to accept that a number of benefits
of full integration may be lost.

Even if we restrict the planning activities to service provision and infrastructure
(ranging across all the infrastructure sectors discussed in Section 4 of this
manual), experience shows that attempts at large scale integrated planning can
get bogged down and become too complex for the various city institutions to
handle. The effect of this is serious; few people take any notice; it becomes too
complex to access the resources needed, and even to work out mechanisms of
management, coordination and disbursement of funds. Whilst local

improvements can still take place, the full benefits which can result from strategic planning are not realised.

## Now read on

Section 2 of the manual addresses the specific issues of local project management in relation to different institutional partners. This is particularly relevant for staff of donor and lending agencies who propose to identify programmes for improving services for the poor in towns and cities in partnership with local institutions and organisations.

## References

WELL, (1998) *Guidance Manual on Water Supply and Sanitation Programmes.*